THE
SOBER
IMPACT

CHARLIE BACKER

Dedicated to my wife Kelly,
thank you for always loving me.

TABLE OF CONTENTS

FOREWORD

Addiction, in its many forms, robs us of our freedom, and without freedom, our dignity is threatened and too often destroyed. We are labeled as an addict and stigmatized as having lost our character and moral compass. The shame builds up to the point we are not sure if we are drinking to take away the shame or if our drinking is creating more shame. And so, the destructive cycle continues, leaving a wake of injury and wounds that will not heal.

Charlie takes us on his journey from addiction to freedom in his autobiography. He speaks to us candidly about what it is like to rationalize why he needed alcohol and why it was not necessary to quit. With vulnerability, he tells us that the inability to say no to alcohol, even when he knew in his heart that it was ruining his marriage, family, career, and health, devastated his dignity. His is an honest narrative of surrendering to the grip that alcohol had on his life and accepting that his brain, with all its cravings, was *running* his life.

In his story, we witness how addiction keeps us acting against our better selves and denying what our addiction is doing to us and to those around us. Charlie takes us to that point when he no longer could rationalize his drinking. Taking that first step to sobriety, Charlie describes vividly and candidly how terrifying was his ambivalence. By surrendering to grace, his life was transformed. He eloquently describes what it is like to live full of grace.

Reading this autobiography will give you a penetrating vision into his struggle with addiction. You will find common threads and unique differences. But undergirding all this is a deep sense of grace. If you read his words and read in between the lines you will see where Charlie's first step transformed his shaming addiction into a life of grace-filled dignity. Charlie invites the reader to take that first step into freedom.

Gary U. Behrman, PhD, MSW, M.Div., LCSW

INTRODUCTION

"I don't typically act like that, I just had too much to drink. It was probably the stress I'm dealing with or the fact that I didn't eat much."

You see, I always found a way to justify my drinking. But deep down I wanted to stop, I tried many times. Until one day, it eventually clicked. This book is about my experiences with sobriety and the adventures of my journey. Sobriety is the greatest gift I never knew I needed, and my life has been greatly transformed because of it.

This book may not make you sober, but if you are looking for the courage and strength to take that first step I hope you can read my experiences, and realize that you are not alone. You can reclaim your life and begin your own transformation.

As I was preparing to write this book, I knew that some chapters would be painful to remember. But, I heard a quote recently that said "If it's not painful to share, you're not being honest with yourself." Whelp, some of these chapters are going to hurt.

I've never been one to beat around the bushes. So get ready to jump right into one of the worst moments of my life.

CHAPTER 1

THE NIGHT I SHOULD HAVE DIED.

"The act of greatness begins with a simple belief in yourself."
~ Charlie Backer

February 24th, 7:20 am

"It's okay. At least you didn't kill anyone," the man next to me said as we were preparing to be released from the Justice Center. I had been arrested for crashing my car into a power line while drunk. I was shaken, destroyed, and humiliated. As I departed, the man turned to me again and said, ", be grateful. God chose to let you live. He wants great things for you." This was February 24th, 2017, three weeks before I chose to live sober.

As I sat in that jail cell alone I was so scared I couldn't stop shaking. I knew that if my past continued to repeat itself, eventually, I figured, I'd either be dead or divorced or in prison. But how could I become sober, if the longest streak

I've had in life was just a few months? I was lost and felt hopeless.

Have you ever been so scared and confused, that you know exactly why you are where you are, but it still doesn't scare you enough to make you change? That's what I felt like after being processed, pictured, and fingerprinted at the justice center. I was sitting in a large area with other people that were arrested that night. The smell was horrid; it was a mixture of urine and body odor. I'm sure there were others there that had been there for hours. The bathroom doors didn't have locks and the pungent smells drifted to where we were sitting. The chairs were hard plastic. I couldn't get comfortable. I was restless, frightened.

I called my wife on the phone. She answered, relieved to hear that I was okay.

Let's rewind that night a bit. Here's where it began:

February, 23rd

The day was a normal one for me. Everything about my life stressed me out. My career, my marriage, my parenting, nothing was going my way. So, when I wrapped up work and shut down my laptop, I headed to my fueling station, which had become a routine stop each evening, to my wife's disappointment. I was having a few drinks with acquaintances, those drinks eventually led me to another get-together. It was already dark and I had been drinking for hours. I decided to head home.

February 23rd, 9:30 PM

I talked to my wife on the phone as I neared our house. I told her I'd be home in a few minutes. Less than a mile away, I hung up the phone.

CLICK

I had driven this road 1000s of times. But, the alcohol had caught up with me. I floored the gas, thinking that I was some hot shot flying down the road to get home. I don't even know what I was thinking. I probably wasn't thinking at all. I blacked out. I remember turning off the road and hitting a mailbox. It felt like a dream. I wasn't in control. I didn't even feel like I was awake.

CRASH

I plowed straight into an electrical pole.

AWAKE

My eyes opened. I could see the dust **from** the airbags flying around the inside of my car. I sat up, still feeling like I was dreaming.

I stepped out of the car and tripped on the ground. I was too drunk to even walk, but I managed to move away from the car. Sparks flew overhead. There was a power line on top of my car. I could see the volts flying all around me. Somehow, I made it to the road, desperately hoping that maybe I'd finally wake up from this nightmare.

The rest of the night was a blur for the most part. I went via ambulance to the hospital to be checked out. As I was in the ambulance I prayed that I'd wake up and it'd all be some sick dream. "I'll change, I promise!", I cried to myself.

My wife followed the ambulance to the hospital and called my friend. They showed up in my room shortly after my arrival.

After being checked out at the hospital, though I had a laceration on my head, all the scans came back fine, and I was told I'd need to go to the justice center to be fingerprinted and processed. Because of my accident, and the presumption that I was drinking while driving, an officer had been stationed at the hospital waiting for my release. As we walked outside, I continued to sober up. With each sobering step, I moved closer to the waiting police car, I became more dreadfully aware of the scope of my evening. I turned to my wife and hugged her.

I jokingly asked the cop if he would let me turn the lights on, to which he said "no." It was my first time in a police car. There I was, in the front seat with handcuffs on.

The police officer was nice. Cordial. He drove me to the justice center. If you've never been arrested before, it's not the most exciting experience. As we neared the justice center, the officer called in our arrival, and a garage door opened on the side of the building. After we parked, he put his duty belt in the trunk, and let me out of the front seat. Still cuffed.

We walked into the building through the garage entrance. I was told to sit, and soon after instructed to remove my shoelaces, and belt, and empty my pockets. I was searched, then sent to be processed by the nurse.

"Next", I heard come from the nurse's room.

As I walked in, filled with disgust, I looked up to see the nurse. I recognized him.

"I'm Charlie Backer, your nephew is my best friend," I said.

"Oh my Charlie, I know who you are."

Though humbling, to see someone I knew in the slightest, gave me an ambivalent sense of both peace and shame. I was quickly checked out and told to wait in the next area.

I shook the officer's hand and thanked him. Deep down I felt that this would be the beginning of something new in my life. I spent the night in jail. My wife picked me up in the morning. My shirt was still bloodied from the crash, serving as a reminder of what happened. She took me to the police station to get my wallet and belongings from the car.

Once I got home I took a shower and immediately crashed onto the bed. I closed my eyes so tight while praying "God, please let this be a dream. Please let me wake up."

I slept for a few hours.

I woke up still painfully hungover, with a splitting headache. I talked to my wife a bit. She was relieved that I was okay. She didn't ask many questions, maybe since she was in as much a state of shock as I was. Or maybe it was anger that kept her quiet, fearful of exploding with all the concerns that had built up over the years?

After I got out of bed, the house was calm. Most of the lights were off. It was early in the afternoon and the kids were still at school. Yet, on the inside, I felt like an erupting volcano.

The nightmare that I lived just a few hours ago, was now a reality...and I was finally coming to terms that it did happen.

As I walked through the house, I wondered what would happen next. What do I even DO in this situation?

I eventually found myself in our garage. I figured I still had a bottle of wine hidden somewhere.

When I couldn't find it, I asked my wife about it. She said calmly, "I got rid of all the alcohol."

I nodded with disappointment. But in my heart, I felt powerless. "Why am I still craving alcohol? I almost died last night, and all I can think about is needing another drink. Damn, do I have a problem?"

Chapter 2

We all have to start somewhere

"You can't go back and change the beginning, but you can start where you are and change the ending."
- C.S Lewis.

The sad truth about my situation is that my car accident didn't make me quit drinking, it only made me stop drinking and driving. In the coming weeks, if I had even one drink, I would insist the other person drive. I surmised in my head that I didn't have a drinking problem. No, it wasn't alcohol's fault that I almost died. It was the fact that I drove a car while drinking. That's the problem, not alcohol.

A logical person that runs his car into a pole, gets arrested, and almost dies because of alcohol, will choose to get sober.

But not me.

Alcohol didn't make me logical.

I continued to make excuses for my drinking.

I continued to drink.

And I drank a lot.

I remember pouring a bottle of wine into a plastic cup and drinking it throughout the evening. My wife had no clue. If she did, she didn't say anything. She innocently trusted me. I didn't act drunk. But I slowly began to realize then that if I can't be honest with myself, how the hell am I supposed to be honest with my wife?

Reflecting on my past

My sober journey didn't begin with one choice to become sober, and then, like a light switch, made me sober. I tried numerous times to quit drinking. I can remember one attempt back in 2015, on a Halloween night, my kids were still so young, that we dressed them up for trick or treating. I made a dip for family and friends to enjoy while we were giving out candy. Even back then I had a gnawing ache that I might have a drinking problem. Several nights I would drink too much. Yet, I'd always find an excuse: I was stressed, I was hungry, I was celebrating. I knew I didn't drink like other people, or, at least I wasn't ready to acknowledge that. But I made excuses and denied that there was a problem. It wasn't out of the norm for me to drink two bottles of wine in an evening, or have multiple vodka tonics. I made a "Charlie drink", which typically entailed a large glass filled with ice, then filled almost 3/4 with vodka, then topped with tonic. It was so strong. Yet, at my height of drinking, the taste of alcohol didn't phase me. It was refreshing.

Back to Halloween night in 2015. I had made a goal to not drink for 30 days just to prove to myself that I was not a drunk and that I did not have a problem with alcohol. But, that night, I felt such boredom. It felt like the evening dragged on forever. A minute felt like an hour. After trick or treating, I went to the kitchen to clean up from the night. One thing I realized with sobriety is that with all the extra energy and attention, sometimes it's easier to keep myself busy cleaning and tidying up just to help the time pass. After I finished cleaning up the kitchen, I remember walking into my living room and seeing my wife, my son, and my daughter all asleep on the couch. I was filled with such gratitude to be sober in that moment. To experience such a beautiful sight in my life to see my family content and exhausted from Halloween, and me, not be drinking. But to be fully present. Thinking of that moment brings tears to my eyes. Alcohol sometimes takes away our ability to see the beauty in the simplest moments of life. Still to this day I look back at the night with such pride, such gratitude. There is peace in the stillness of life.

Alcohol Lies

One of the false claims I believed about alcohol, was that it defined and empowered me. I'm a pretty sociable person, but deep down I struggled with anxiety and a lack of confidence. Whenever I would arrive at parties, I would make sure that my vodka was ready. I had a big glass in hand, took a drink, and would think, "Ahh, now I can relax." I thought that alcohol gave me strength. I thought it made me who I was supposed to be. I thought it gave me confidence, it made me funny, and it made me more attractive. It would take many extremely humbling and embarrassing moments to finally see how alcohol was betraying me and breaking every promise it ever made to me. Yet I was unable to take the right steps toward sobriety. Alcohol was in control of my life and my decisions. Not only was alcohol betraying me, but I was also in the depths of betraying myself and all those I loved.

People say "when life hands you lemons, you make lemonade." But, what do I do when I believe that my world is crumbling because of my stupid mistakes?

I was feeling all sorts of emotions following the night of my car accident. Feelings of: fear, shame, humiliation, doubt. I knew that these emotions were not going to diminish and I began believing that alcohol would ease them, maybe even erase them. Just one drink of vodka and all would go away and I would feel better. These intense feelings that accompanied every waking hour and even into the dark recesses of my nighttime dreams persisted. I felt like I had this huge hole to climb out of. I knew how to dig that hole, but I had little knowledge or conviction in how to climb out.

I can remember one of the first times I tried to live sober. I was filled with so much fear and anxiety. Specifically, thoughts of my past would cripple me into a depressed state, or I'd lock myself in my room and pray that sleep would let me forget. I still hung on to the belief that alcohol alone would make it all go away. But, the reality is that we all do stupid things. And, for me when I was drinking, there were plenty of moments that I wish I could forget or change. When I took alcohol out of my life, it forced me to face my fears and confront my past head-on. I had to stop believing that alcohol was my friend who could get me through any emotion that would be unbearable. I didn't know how to live with excruciating uncomfortable emotions. How was I going to do this without alcohol?

Understanding I have a problem

Google is a great place to start to figure out answers. I remember researching sobriety online in hopes of finding an answer to why I couldn't have just one drink. I would do online quizzes with titles like, "Am I an alcoholic?", or "Do I have a drinking problem?". I Googled sobriety so frequently that I'd find myself reading the same articles over and over again. But, no matter what I read, it never clicked that I should (or even could) be sober.

When I was drinking alcohol, I would plan out my evening drinking before I even got home. Do I have enough vodka? Do I have bottles of wine stashed in the garage? Will I run out? I always wanted to make sure I had "enough".

One of the first realizations that I had a problem with alcohol, was watching a hockey game on tv at home with my wife. By the 2nd period I looked at my nearly empty bottle of wine and wondered if I open another bottle, will it last me through the game? Can I finish it before bed?

As the game ended, I picked up my two empty bottles of wine, cleaned up, and got ready to go upstairs. I then picked up my wife's beer. She had opened it at the beginning of the game, and here we were a few hours later and she barely drank half of it. I distinctly remember thinking at the time: Why can't I be like my wife? Why can't I only have one drink?

I believe that our conscience acts as a compass for our bodies. It typically tells us when we've had enough to drink, and we stop. Yet, for me, I didn't have that ability to self-moderate. The real truth here is that there was never enough for me. I had to acknowledge that my alcohol use was probably hiding the fact that I was struggling with some internal issues, past trauma, or stress that seemed so overwhelming that it was best to numb my emotions. Alcohol promised to do this if I agreed to its terms: More! More! More is better and I want more!

The glimpses of freedom during the struggle

I had glimpses of an alcohol-free future during my journey to be sober. It's tempting at times to view a sober journey as starting once I commit and I'm successful, but it takes time. We're not built like light switches, I can't simply flip a switch and become sober. Maybe that's the case for some, but in my experience, it took many, many tries. For me, it was like learning to ride my bike – it took several attempts before I knew how to ride a bike. But, the funny thing is that I don't look back and remember the times I fell off the bike. The falls were part of the process of learning to ride. I relish the times I got back up. The feeling of riding without training wheels, the freedoms I gave myself by not giving up. Now I could explore new places and create new adventures on my bike.

Years before I got sober, I was in a phase of trying to either limit how much alcohol I would drink or not drink at all. I wasn't ready to commit to a life without alcohol. So, I made it my goal not to drink for 30 days, like that Halloween night years prior.

I wanted to be sober. I was looking for reasons to explain my sobriety and found that the goal of not drinking, helped.

The difference between that phase of not drinking for a time and my now successful journey toward lifelong sobriety is the belief I now hold that I don't need alcohol. In early attempts to stop drinking, I felt that I was taking something good out of my life. It took me many tries at sobriety to not only accept that it was the best way for me to move forward, but that alcohol is not good for me. Since I chose sobriety, I didn't feel like I was giving up anything. Alcohol was taking so much from me, I lost myself to alcohol, but giving it up gave me my life back.

Here is what I had to ask myself to see if I had a drinking problem: Feel free to ask yourself these same questions

- Have I had times when I drank more than I intended?
- Have I tried to reduce or quit alcohol multiple times with little to no success?
- Have I spent a lot of time drinking or being sick from the aftereffects?
- Have I wanted a drink so badly you couldn't think of anything else?
- Has drinking often interfered with work, family, or school?
- Have I continued to drink alcohol even though it was causing trouble with my family or friends?
- Have I given up or cut back on activities to drink?

- Have I gotten into situations while or after consuming alcohol that increased my chances of getting hurt?
- Have I continued to drink alcohol even though it was making me feel depressed, anxious, or after not remembering the night before?
- Do I need to drink much more than I once did to get the effect I want? Or found that the usual number of drinks had much less effect?

CHAPTER 3

WHEN EVERYTHING CLICKED

"Every journey begins with a single step."
Mayo Angelou

I remember it like it was yesterday. The date was March 19th, 2017; it was a Sunday evening. My wife and I were at a friend's wedding reception. There was an open bar. We got a round of drinks and sat down. As the music played and speeches went by, I felt something different inside me. I felt a voice telling me, this will be the last time you'll ever drink. I wasn't scared like times before. I didn't immediately run to the bar and ask for five double vodka tonics. As I sipped the two drinks I had for the night, I pondered what my future would be like. My nerves didn't run up inside me and tell me that I'm going to fail, that I'll never make it. No, I had an overwhelming sense of peace. I didn't say anything to my wife about it that night. I had failed to get sober so many times in the past, and the last thing I wanted to do was let anyone down.

After the wedding, I remember lying in bed thinking to myself, "I wonder what is ahead?" It's a question many of us ask ourselves time and time again. What is waiting for us beyond the next turn? Where will we go after this? In truth: no one knows. But, in my heart, I knew that if my years of abusing alcohol could teach me anything, it's that if I keep drinking and repeating the mistakes of the past, my life would be filled with pain, regret, humiliation, and unhealthy behaviors.

The first day

It was a cold March day. It was raining. I drove to work, contemplating the certainty that I would never drink again. I didn't question sobriety the first day. I think, all the past failures and attempts had finally collided in my mind, and it was my heart's way of saying "That's enough."

I decided to go to an AA meeting. I found one a few minutes away at an old church. I walked in, filled with anxiety. Will they judge me? Will I feel worse than I do now? What is going to happen? I can still remember the smell of freshly brewed coffee in that dingy conference room. The room was set up with chairs in a circle. I sat down, not making eye contact with anyone. I'm a sociable person, but at that moment, though I had a hunger for a sober life, I was burdened with guilt and shame from past failures. After sitting for a while, the meeting started. They went around the circle and everyone introduced themselves. When they came around to me, I spoke without emotion, "My name is Charlie.....and I'm an alcoholic." It was the first and last words spoken by me at that meeting. I had been denying that I was an alcoholic for too long. Even as I write this, I would still rather say that I abused alcohol than saying that I'm an alcoholic. I sat in the meeting and listened as others shared their stories and read from the big book. In case you haven't been to an AA meeting, the Big Book is the core principle that they often read at every meeting. After the meeting was over, I stood up and I saw an older member walk up to the person leading the meeting. He bought a copy of the Big Book and gave it to me as well as a few others to read. I said thanks and walked to my car with an overwhelming sense of peace. I was as excited then as I was the night of the wedding when I held that vodka drink and knew it would be my last. I wasn't worried so much about the future at that moment. I was just going to take it one day at a time.

I think the weather that first day helps explain how my brain was the first few weeks. Rainy. Foggy. Unclear. I didn't have a plan in my head for "How to be a Sober Charlie". But I had the belief that sobriety could make me better than I currently was.

That afternoon I called a psychologist and set an appointment for the next day.As the day went on I knew that if I wanted to remain sober, I'd have to begin making other changes in my life, not just eliminating alcohol.

When I came home, I told my wife about my day. For the first time in a long time, I uttered the words, "I'm done with drinking. I don't know what to do." It felt right. Peace and joy engulfed me as my wife gave me a huge hug.

Journaling

I've always been an avid fan of journaling. Through different phases of my life I'd jot down how my life was going, or anything new, difficult, or exciting that was happening. In my desire to push myself to get sober, I created a folder on my phone called "Regrettable moments with drinking". While this wasn't something I took track of while I was drinking, during my sobering phase I would write down certain events that popped into my head that I regretted. The pain of regret that I struggled with while drinking and during sobriety was horrible. I'm not sure what to relate it to but, imagine the emotions of embarrassment, dread, and humiliation all rolled into one feeling, that's the regret I'm referring to.

Denial is at the core of alcohol abuse. So journaling helped me not only write about those past experiences, but also the emotions that I felt at that moment. These records ended up being very helpful, especially later on whenever I was having a moment of temptation or wanted to look back at how things used to be and start believing again that it wasn't that bad.

I can promise you, that you will never, ever, wake up in the morning and regret not drinking the night before. Instead, you will wake up grateful for another night of sobriety.

These are some of the changes I made early in my sober journey:

- Removed alcohol from my house
- Told those closest to me that I'm sober
- Prayed about who I could turn to for support and asked for their support
- Researched sober topics
- Avoided places where I would have typically gone to drink
- Avoided people I felt pressured to drink around
- Talked to a doctor about my choice to become sober
- Drank a lot of water
- Stayed active: I joined a local gym and set the goal of working out at least once a week.

- Created a list of things to do to fill the void that was left when alcohol was gone (I realized quite quickly how much time I gained each day)

CHAPTER 4

THINGS THAT JUST MAKE SENSE WHEN YOU BECOME SOBER

"Don't say what a good man should be, be one."
Marcus Aurelius

As I look back at my life, I found myself focusing on what I HOPED was ahead of me. To live in a world where I didn't have to wake up with a feeling of regret in the morning. I prayed that I'd no longer have to worry about what I said or did the night before. I would no longer have to worry about blacking out and forgetting. I'd become a father whom my kids would think of without always picturing a drink in my hand. I'd become an ever-present husband that is there to protect and love his wife, and together we'd help each other to be better. That I could focus on being the best me, and taking care of myself physically, mentally, and spiritually.

Change cannot happen without choice.

The choice is meaningless without action.

Now it is your time to choose. There are probably many fears flying through your head right now. Will I still be myself? Will people still like me? Will I still like myself? Will I lose friends? Will I be happy?

A big concern or change that one experiences early on in the sober journey is the fear of the "what if". Because you are choosing a path that you haven't been on before, there are many questions about what will happen in life. During this phase, one can experience high levels of anxiety or discomfort. But, don't be afraid, this is only temporary.

In sobriety, I was always trying to visualize things. What would the future be like? How would I be? I eventually got the vision that I was walking on a path through a deep forest. I passed by the usual trees, everything seemed familiar, it felt safe, it felt like home. As I stepped further into the forest I arrived at a fork in the road. On the left, I saw the familiar path I'd traveled before, the high points and the low points, the pretty spots and the dangerous corners. To my right, I saw a path I'd never walked on before. I was intrigued by the challenge, and yet afraid of what was beyond.

I think we can all acknowledge that our future can seem a bit unknown. And, when I was becoming sober, I struggled so much with not wanting to give up alcohol, not wanting to change. Yet, I knew that if I wanted to achieve anything better for myself, I had to make the step toward it. I think we all must make a choice at which fork we will take in life. We must weigh the knowns and unknowns, the fears and the hopes, the realities, and the past, and make that first step.

Things to ask yourself:

- Has my drinking brought me closer to or farther away from those I love?
- Am I proud of the person I am when I'm drinking?
- Do I want to be better?
- Am I willing to sacrifice some temporary discomfort in the belief that there is freedom out there I have yet to experience?

At this point of the early sober journey, drill down to know WHY you're wanting to become sober. Ingrain it in your brain. The path you choose is going to dictate the future you have. If you go on the path you've gone before, you can expect to keep answering those previous questions in the same fashion forever. Yet, if you go the other path you are preparing to go the road less traveled.

The reality of choice is that what happens next is never a guarantee. Yet, if we can remember our why, and acknowledge where we HOPE to be, that's all that we can do.

What do I drink?

I was a big fan of wine and vodka tonics. When I chose to get sober, I went out and bought a few cases of sparkling mineral water in several flavors and loaded my fridge up. Instead of just giving up the vodka tonics and leaving a void

I could potentially try to fill in a moment of weakness, I replaced those former favorites with something healthy and refreshing, and it helped. I eventually settled on plain San Pellegrino's, and sometimes water with lemons in it.

Adjusting to going out without a drink in my hand

This part was hard. For a long period of my life (before having kids) we would go out regularly and meet with friends at a local restaurant for drinks. I think at that point in my life I viewed alcohol and socialization as hand in hand. Being sober meant I had to go out into the world without a drink to give me a buzz and help me be sociable. It took some getting used to.

During the first few months of my sobriety, I avoided a lot of people. I avoided places where I drank before. Over time, if I did go out, I had the impression that people would see my sobriety as some sort of sickness. "Oh Charlie's sober, don't anyone drink around him!" I projected judgment from my friends upon myself, but in reality, my insecurities were pushing through.

I've already talked about how I'd come to realize that alcohol for me had become a crutch. I could blame my bad behavior on the drink. I could blame stupid statements on the alcohol. But I'd also attribute great things to drinking.

"Oh, it's only because of the vodka that you asked her out." "It's only because of alcohol that people like you." They were all lies. I had to make a real shift to believing that I didn't need that crutch and that I could be great and do great things without alcohol.

For every excuse that I had for my drinking, there was an excruciating pain that filled my being the morning after. It's one thing to experience this feeling of shame and regret once, but it's another thing to have it on repeat. And, the worst of it was not remembering much of the night before at all. WHY DO I KEEP DOING THIS?

In the early days, if I did go out in public, I would order a club soda with lime. I would hide my sobriety for fear of others judging me. Eventually, I stopped this. Eventually, I didn't care. But in the early days and months of sobriety, it took me some time to get acclimated to the world.

Boredom No More

One thing that I wasn't prepared for in sobriety was boredom. I didn't realize how many nights I wasted away drinking, that when I finally got sober, I didn't know what to do with all the time on my hands.

I am a person that is pained by boredom. I like to be busy, or feel productive. But the boredom helped me to acknowledge that I used alcohol as a drug. I struggled to address my anxiety and stress of life and found solace in drinking till I felt nothing.

Someone once said if you want to figure out what you're avoiding in life, put down your drink. It was about the idea that many people who abuse alcohol, are using it to avoid an area of their life.

FOMO: Fear of Missing Out

During the first weeks and months of sobriety, the fear of missing out was huge. I was afraid so much in the beginning: of not being invited out, not seeing my friends, not hanging out with people. I had a fear of being abandoned. I will say that the FOMO hurt at times.

The sober journey can be so scary, especially in the beginning. That's when I realized that I needed the most support and encouragement from those closest to me. More specifically, it needs to be positive support, and many of those "drinking buddies" may not be there to cheer you on unless there's a shot glass in their hand.

The pain of the transition to sobriety stung at times. I was learning to step out in the world as a different person, almost like a caterpillar turning into a butterfly. I knew I was changing – I could feel it and see it, and those closest to me saw it as well.

I learned that what may be transparent to me and my support group may not be apparent to anyone else. It's like what they say about working out and eating healthy: you begin to see physical changes in the first month, your close friends see it after a few months, and other people will notice it many months later. Just because people cannot see that you changed, doesn't mean that you haven't. My sobriety wasn't based on or determined by anyone else's belief but my own. The reality was that the FOMO will eventually subside, but until then I had to be focused on becoming a better person. This required me to be focused on self-caring, and that's okay. When I focus on myself, it allows me to become the best person, and then I can share that with the world. Until then, don't be afraid to stay inside, keep your friend groups small, and decline invitations to go out. Do what you believe you need to do to attain, maintain and excel at your sobriety. That's what worked for me, and in the next few chapters, I'll share more detail about how I did it.

CHAPTER 5

FINDING SUPPORT

"It's okay, to not be okay"
Fr. Brian Fallon

Initially, I didn't know what to do to become sober. I had tried so many times to get sober in the past, and I felt as though if I tried those ways again, I would end up back where I began. This time I took it one day at a time. I began meeting with a psychologist, who not only helped me in continuing to be sober but helped me to realize WHY I was drinking so much. Had I never placed myself in the position to be open to meeting with a doctor, I may have never been successful with my sobriety.

You may be wondering how I came to find a psychologist. Well, let me be honest first: some stigmas exist. I've felt them greatly when trying to deal with depression, anxiety, and sobriety. The stigma with sobriety is that we shouldn't tell anyone we're not perfect. I was so afraid to tell my doctor how I was feeling. Yet, I knew deep down that I had something to share inside me, that I couldn't explain. I knew that if I wanted to pursue sobriety, I needed to change. Gratefully I had friends in my life that had experience with psychologists. They helped me to figure out how to search online for doctors that took my insurance. I found one that looked appealing. She seemed nice from her picture, and it said she specialized in working with those who abuse alcohol.

With the help of these medical professionals, I was able to understand that oftentimes alcoholic behavior, or the inclination to abuse alcohol, stems from trauma in life, external stresses, or issues beyond our control. Professional outside support during this phase is extremely enlightening and helpful in charting a new path towards being sober. If you are on your way to starting your sober journey, I highly recommend that you have a conversation with your family doctor about your health, and consider going to see a psychologist.

In addition to a psychologist or doctor, it is imperative that you have a personal support group of people who will encourage you and not be a source of temptation. There are so many things changing in the beginning, you'll need your spouse, closest friends, or family members to be a solid foundation for you, to encourage you, or simply share a prayer with you to get you through the day.

With that support, once you've rid your life of alcohol and all the people whom you'd feel pressure to drink around, you can begin to rebuild. You can fill in those spaces left by those you had to push out. Take heart that some of the changes you have to make initially are not necessarily forever. Honestly, for myself, I enjoyed having a few drinks and playing cards with my friends. When I became sober, I knew I had to put this on hold. I was afraid that I'd lose those friends. I was afraid that I'd lose myself. But, as years went on, I realized that the "stepping away" part of sobriety was only temporary. But, the reality is that you need to protect yourself as you're beginning to explore the world for the first time.

There are plenty of formal support group options out there like Alcoholics Anonymous, SMART Recovery, LifeRing, Church groups, and others.

7 tips for finding support:

1. Talk to those closest to you

2. Search out a doctor

3. Speak to your priest or pastor

4. Go to an AA or SMART meeting

5. Search online for support tools

6. Read about sobriety

7. Find like-minded people

CHAPTER 6

LEANING ON FAITH TO NAVIGATE THE UNKNOWN

"Be who God meant you to be and you will set the world on fire."
St. Catherine of Sienna

There are some things I can't explain. I've replayed the night of my accident over in my mind a million times. Early on, the feelings I had were shame and humiliation. But, as time has gone by, it's shifted to gratitude. I firmly believe that I survived that accident solely by the grace of God. After crashing into the pole, with the electrical wires flailing all about the top of my car and around me, I felt as though an angel was lifting them up so that I could walk to safety.

I don't know if that's what happened. But that's what it felt like.

Before we dig deeper, let me explain a little about my past which has always been a huge part of my life. I studied to be a Catholic priest for several years. My spirituality, and my faith, are the foundation by which I stand each day. I don't press my views upon others but have found that faith has empowered me to be the man that I am today.

Here's a flashback to give you detail:

Hugs are not something I do often. Yet, still in my life, there are certain hugs that I will remember forever. My mother passed away several years ago from cancer. Before she realized she was sick, I remember her giving me the greatest hug ever, trying to console me. I had been sick with some unknown illness for a few months. I was worried about life, my new family, and everything. In that hug, I felt total peace and comfort. After she passed away I felt empty, I felt alone, and I felt like a part of me died. A few days before her funeral I got a hug from someone else. It was someone I had only met in passing, and she said "come here, give me a hug." The warmth I felt was overwhelming. I think that's what faith can be to us. It is hope in our darkest moments. It is comfort when we feel alone. It is an answer in a confusing phase.

My choice to leave a world of alcohol abuse, and shift to a life of sobriety was a miraculous moment in my life. I like the definition of insanity: Doing the same things over and over again, expecting different results. I felt like I was lost in this cycle of drinking that knew no end. Yet, leaning on faith helped to lift the burden sometimes found in sobriety, especially in the early times.

To do things you've never done, you must be willing to chart a path never explored.

I have always been a spiritual person. I was raised by a mother who always spoke about the saints, prayed the rosary, and showed me what true faith was. Yet, when I struggled with alcohol, I felt as though my prayers weren't being answered. Had I done something wrong? How can I change? I needed help on this journey, and by the grace of God, I was blessed to have a wonderful spiritual director who walked this path with me and allowed me to see God at work even in my darkest days. I remember meeting with my spiritual director and telling her everything that had transpired with my drinking, and that I felt God calling me to be sober. It was another vulnerable moment. Yet, I felt freedom at that moment. The same way a small child feels the warmth of their parent when they run into their bedroom after having a nightmare. Peace in the crashing waves of life may not always be attainable through our desire but in the cooperation of others.

The area that I've probably leaned on the most in my sobriety is faith. I can explain time and time again what exactly I did to become sober. I explain the steps I took, the things I eliminated from my life, and the books I read, but that doesn't scratch the surface.

How does one explain faith?

Sometimes you just know that things will work out. It may go against logic to believe that the cyclical motion of addiction and pain can stop. But it's true. While I focus so much on the logical choice or the rational explanation, I must say that it is by the grace of God that I'm sober. When I didn't know where else to turn, I knew I could pray, I could visit a church, I could sit with the Lord. Faith played the role of adding calm to the rumbling waves that were rocking my life. My faith became my foundation.

It's easy to fall into the temptation that EVERYTHING must be perfect for us to succeed at something. But the reality is, that we're imperfect beings, and we need to be logical with our goals and aspirations. By placing my faith in God to carry me when I could not walk and to lead me when I could not see helped. I'm not saying the path was easy, but relying on faith allowed me to focus on that which I could control.

CHAPTER 7

CHANGE HAPPENS SO SLOWLY, YET SO QUICKLY.

*"Today you are You, that is truer than true. There is no one alive
who is Youer than You,"*
Dr. Seuss

A few months into my sober journey I began to experience something like being reborn. It felt like I was shedding the past, and embarking on a future with new vigor, new perspective, and above all, newfound freedom from toxic behavior.

Gone were the mornings of fear and regret, and now was a time of joy and peace…knowing that I had a new lease on life.

I think a way to relate to this feeling is for you to think back to when you were a kid getting ready to start the first day of school. You had the summer to be "you", to have fun with friends and family, and experience things differently than those in your class. I remember being SO excited about my first day returning to school after a summer break from high school. I would call some of my classmates the night before to express this excitement. I was excited to see people, but also because I knew I had changed, I had grown.

On my sober journey, fears and anxiety eventually did subside, and I was filled with an awesome feeling of accomplishment. At this point, I was well on my way to creating proper boundaries with other people and setting expectations for my life ahead.

Going public

It took me two years to start opening up publicly about my sobriety. I never really accepted that I was sober. Maybe I had imposter syndrome. But, early on, I was taking it one day at a time. Yet, even though I could see the days go by, or the months add up, it took me a few years to acknowledge that I was sober.

I think that's part of a lie that we tell ourselves in the beginning, or at least that's what I told myself. During the early days of sobriety, I was still coming off a life of being a people pleaser. So to shift from that to a sober person, meant that I was taking action for myself, and not for others. Early on in sobriety, we don't know the person that we will become, we don't know how sobriety will change us. And it was this thinking that made me question: Am I really sober? I know it sounds silly. Heck, typing that felt off. But it's true. Sobriety, especially for those whose lives were so intertwined with alcohol, felt foreign. Finally, after some time had passed, and thanks to weekly therapy sessions, I was able to accept that I was sober and that I had changed my life for the better.

Early on I started a short-lived podcast where I explained my experiences with getting sober, my struggles, my wins, my high moments, and my lows. It was called The Sober Charlie Podcast. And, I had an Instagram that I used to post sober memes and quotes. Over the course of a few months, my social media following skyrocketed from just a few hundred to thousands of followers. In every post and every podcast, I would share more about my journey. And, while I initially started doing them to share my experiences with the world, I quickly realized that The Sober Charlie Podcast had become an outlet for me to deal with becoming sober. Eventually, I stopped posting altogether. I still have the recordings on a computer at home. But, I view that moment of my sober journey as a phase of therapy that allowed me to externalize the feelings I had inside.

I felt like I was reborn when I became sober. I had to relearn a lot of things, and I got to have so many new experiences as a sober person that I didn't fully acknowledge the first time around.

It's interesting to discuss sobriety publicly. When I shared my podcast or shared posts on social media, my inboxes were flooded with people seeking advice, wanting help, and needing direction. I didn't feel I was doing anything special by sharing my experiences, but reality showed me very quickly that there are so many people out there hurting. They just need to feel validated and know that they can get better. Sobriety affects everyone, and the more we can be there to build others up, the better off we will be. I created a photo album on my phone labeled "It's not me, It's God." In it, I would screenshot all of the positive messages and requests for help that flooded my inboxes.

"There is good in store for you", I would tell myself almost daily as I woke up each morning without a hangover. I tried for a long time to put into words how I was feeling. Becoming sober can at times, feel like jumping into a hurricane. I felt like I was being hit from everywhere while I'm moving along life, changing, evolving. Yet, through that crazy whirlwind, something magical happens. I found out who I truly was, and in that, I was able to share myself more fully with the world.

It puts a smile on my face to watch my kids grow up. They're in grade school now, but I'm their dad. I can play with them, sing with them, pray with them, and watch movies with them. I can do anything I want with them as their dad. Sobriety allowed me to be the best dad I can be for them. One of the greatest gifts that sobriety gives you is the ability to be fully present to those around you, especially those closest to you.

My kids may not remember the days when I used to drink, but I can promise you that I won't be creating any new memories that revolve around my drinking. They will have an ever-present and loving father who wants the best for them and is going to do everything in his power to be that for them. Sobriety isn't just a choice, it's an active verb that doesn't just start or stop on demand; it goes on forever. It requires your attention, your strength, your focus. But in return, you're given a freedom and energy that was totally unavailable to the person you were before you were sober.

After healing, your other relationships in life will improve. I didn't realize how much alcohol was stopping me from being a present dad and husband. Once becoming sober, I began to live gratefully in the day-to-day moments of life with joy. Watching my son's soccer game. Watching my daughter at gymnastics. It's beautiful.

Here are some of the concrete changes I saw as I evolved into my sober self:

- I became healthier
- I became more productive
- My energy increased

- I felt more present and therefore able to appreciate my life
- I had more time to do the things I wanted
- I didn't wake up with regrets from the night before
- I had more control over my behavior
- I slept better

CHAPTER 8

LEARNING TO FULLY BE MYSELF

"When we least expect it, life tests our willingness to change; at such a moment, there is no point in saying that we are not ready."
Paulo Coelho

Things change. When we make a choice as a child to stop riding our bikes with training wheels, our world changes. Suddenly we're able to go faster, cut sharper turns, and hang out with the cool kids. When one chooses to become sober, there are a lot of things that change. Almost like the first experience on your brand new bike, the new adventure of your life is about, to begin with, you FULLY present for every moment.

The summer after I graduated from high school I cycled my bike from the St. Louis Arch to Toronto Canada to see Pope John Paul II. At this point in my life, I was studying to be a Catholic priest and was joined on this journey by priests and other seminarians. I can remember the difficulty of cycling every single day. I remember crossing the Canadian border and getting free hot dogs from a stand. We were almost to Toronto, and we stopped at a restaurant for dinner. In Canada, the drinking age was 19, so being the youngest in the group, I was the only one who couldn't drink. After everyone ordered their meal and drinks, I remember it coming to me, and the waitress asked how old I was. "18". Unfortunately, due to the rules at this restaurant, everyone had to be 19 or older. Without missing a beat, one of the priests said "well I guess none of us will drink then, pass the menu!". And we went somewhere else.

Drinking has become so common in our life, that we feel that by removing it, we will miss out on something. As I remember back to that warm summer day in Canada many years ago, I don't regret not being able to drink. I don't miss being able to have a beer with my fellow riders. No, I appreciate the boldness of that priest to say "All right, we're leaving." It was as if he was saying we're all a team. We're all together in this.

It's okay to be vulnerable

I'm a pretty private person. While I do have attributes that would lead one to believe I'm an extrovert, I prefer time alone, reading, writing, or meditating on life. I went to my psychologist six months before my sobriety. I went to her initially because I was struggling with drinking, as well as stress, and the recent passing of my mother. When I went to her after the wedding moment, it was different. I started the visit by proclaiming "I quit drinking". She could see something was different about me. She congratulated me on my choice, and we began to dive deeper. After the coming appointments, we discussed a lot of things. My past, my desires, my life, my goals. I came to realize that I was using alcohol to self-medicate. I struggled with social anxiety for a long time and didn't know it. I blamed my anxiety on being awkward, too quiet, or not sociable. I blamed my lack of desire to be sociable on myself. That I wasn't good enough. That I was weak. That I was a failure. That I had something wrong with me. Yet, through therapy, I realized that I struggled with social anxiety, and didn't have the coping mechanisms to deal with it more healthily. I had turned to alcohol to numb the anxiety.

I went through phases with vulnerability. For too long I viewed being vulnerable as being weak. So I hid so much of myself from the world for fear of haters, or toxic people attacking me. Over time, I began to embrace my failings as opportunities to improve. I believe that alcohol allows us to mask so many emotions, so many moments of life, and numb our experiences that we get accustomed to it, almost as if it's a shield. But the shield is a lie. It's a lie that wants you to hide who you are; it wants you to avoid saying things for fear of others looking at you less, it wants you to FEAR the unknown. Eventually, you'll get to point of freedom in vulnerability where you no longer have to hide, but rather, you can embrace it. Being vulnerable allows you to express yourself to the world in such an intimate way. And to those that would attack vulnerabilities, they are weak, pathetic, and toxic individuals who should have nothing to do with your life. Negative people exist. But, your path of sobriety and vulnerability, has within it so much potential to make the world a better place, and positively impact the lives of others.

Advice on dealing with toxic people, places, or things:

We all know there will be people that come and go from our lives, and I found this especially true as I phased from being a drinker to being sober. It wasn't the most fun realization that some of the people I hung out with weren't my friends, but rather just drinking buddies. These people were present in my life to drink and party with me, but without the alcohol, there was no real substance to the relationship. This was a painful discovery. Throughout my process of becoming sober, through meetings with my psychologist and reading books, I discovered that I didn't have healthy boundaries in many areas of my life. So as I was becoming sober, I was always having to redefine healthy boundaries for myself around others, who gets access to me at what time, etc. When I was drinking, I had the desire to be liked by everyone. This may have been fun for other people, but this didn't help me in becoming better. As I grew through sobriety, I became more self-aware of who I am, what I like and don't like, what attracts me, what excites me, and what turns me off. Getting to know myself like this was a fascinating part of the journey. But I acknowledge that it hurt when I lost some friends and let some relationships fade away.

As I matured and walked further along this path, I became more aware of the type of people I wanted to surround myself with. And, I found myself attracting those people in my life.

CHAPTER 9

IS THE GRASS GREENER ON THE SOBER SIDE OF THE FENCE?

"How long are you going to wait before you demand the best for yourself. "Epictetus

I have always been a dreamer when it comes to goals. I can get pretty passionate and focused when it comes to achieving things in my life. Yet, for the longest time I felt that no matter what I did, there were certain things that I couldn't achieve. For instance, I always wanted to have a low body fat with visible abs. I always thought that my genetics were stopping me from achieving a chiseled six-pack. The reality? My use of alcohol stopped me from being able to focus enough on diet and fitness to make any noticeable changes in my life. A few years after becoming sober I made it my goal to get fit. Just like starting my journey to sobriety, I took it one day at a time. Honestly, one push-up at a time.

That led to one mile at a time. To one meal at a time. I eventually found myself looking at the before and after pictures of someone that had dropped 35 pounds and nearly 13% body fat. Was it easy? No. But it was another building block along the mountain of sobriety that I could stand on, knowing that I did it. I changed, and I achieved my goal.

So much time for new activities:

I used to drink almost every evening. I would pour my first drink by 7, and then not stop till I went to bed. When I removed alcohol from my life, I suddenly had hours of extra time in my days. I realized a few days in that not only was my use of alcohol hurting me, it was robbing me of my life. Alcohol made me zone out and miss hours of my life, every day. I have this internal desire to be productive as frequently as possible. I struggled with that desire as a drinker, though the alcohol eliminated any chance of being very productive. Right before getting sober, some friends encouraged me to start selling a hot sauce I had been making at home. So, I made a Facebook page and began selling bottles. At this point, I was making them in my home kitchen and pouring them into mason jars. I remember going from store to store to make sure I had enough bottles and ingredients.

In my sobriety, I gave my attention and energy to creating the hot sauce. After I perfected my new recipe, I went from selling 5 bottles a week to nearly fifty. I soon realized that I couldn't keep making the sauce and selling it from home. I had no experience in making hot sauce or marketing and selling retail food, but I had a belief that others would enjoy my passion-made sauce. Over the next few months, I met with manufacturers, designers, and creative minds to help launch my company, Hot Charlie's. Hot Charlie's officially went commercial a few months later. It's funny, I had no prior experience in cooking. Heck, at that time of my life, I could barely make mac and cheese for my kids without burning it. Yet, I was able to create a hot sauce for retail. I remember thinking "What have I done", as I watched hundreds of bottles flow across the manufacturing line.

Hot Charlie's, has now scaled into offering multiple sauces, many seasonings, spicy popcorn, and spicy frozen pizzas. I know for a fact that had I not gotten sober, Hot Charlie's never would have left my kitchen. Alcohol has a great way of dampening spirits, shifting goals, and making people take the easier road.

I'm grateful for the extra time and energy that sobriety gave to each and every one of my days. For without it, I never would have been able to do such awesome things. Things that I would have never thought possible before.

Healthy

One thing I never took into account with my drinking was how many empty calories were in each drink. I thought of myself as a pretty healthy person. I always had a gym membership. I always had goals. I remember when I was still drinking, I had written in my journal that one day I want to be healthy. I want to feel good. I want to look good. I want health and fitness to be the main part of my life. But, this never became a reality while I was drinking. No matter how focused I was, as soon as someone mentioned taking a shot, I knew my night was going to be spent drinking and eating tons of bar food.

I took a picture of my worst day. Of what I looked like. It captured my feelings of myself: depressed, humiliated, empty.

For each year, as I would celebrate my sobriety, I'd post a side-by-side picture of then and now. In my first year of sobriety, without going to the gym, I lost almost 30 pounds. 30 POUNDS! That is a ton of weight. In the years since I've transitioned to making health and fitness a focal point of my life. I work out consistently and aim to eat as best as I can (while still enjoying a fair amount of Nutella).

Looking back, I could never have imagined life could be the way it is. While I had the goal to one day be healthy and fit, in my drunken state, I could never view my life without alcohol. Alcohol is so misleading.

Being Present

One thing I never realized before sobriety was how alcohol took away quality time spent with those around me. Once I stopped drinking, I realized how much more free time I had. Yes, I got bored at times. Yes, I put energy towards Hot Charlie's and my fitness, but above all: sobriety made me a more present person.

I can remember it like it was yesterday. My son was only 6 or 7. I recently connected my old N64 to the TV and was teaching him to play 007 Goldeneye. If you're in my generation, this game was the bomb when I was growing up. As I sat there playing with him, I took a deep breath and looked around. Time felt like it slowed down. I realized in that short moment that I was being 100% present to my son. I rarely got that feeling when I was still drinking.

But at that moment, I was there, sitting on the couch in my basement with my dog. Playing with my son, while my daughter played with her barbies behind me. It was a surreal moment that reminded me of that Halloween night many years prior. That moment was ingrained in my mind, reminiscent of my wife and kids fast asleep on the couch. Now, fast forward several years, and here I am, gratefully sober. Present. Being a dad. There was so much peace at that moment.

Being Genuine

Becoming sober meant that I had to face the world head-on, as myself, without alcohol as my buffer. This was frighteningly vulnerable for me in the early days. Now, as I look back at my sobriety, those fears of needing alcohol to be myself are completely gone. Sobriety has empowered me to be myself, all the time. A few years into my sobriety I took on the motto of life that vulnerability was one of the greatest skills. The vulnerability allows one to be themselves, without taking into account the fears and thoughts of the world. As I mentioned earlier in the book, I went through a phase where I had a short-lived podcast where I discussed my sobriety. It was during this time that I realized that I didn't have to hide in the shadows because I had a drinking problem. I took charge and took control of my life. I decided that I could stand on my own two feet, and proclaim to the world that I was sober. As this grew throughout my mind and my life over the years, I can't help but be so incredibly grateful to be sober. Though I viewed sobriety as a weakness, and alcohol as a strength, it turned out to be the exact opposite.

Sharing again

Nearly two years after I shuttered the podcast, I began posting about sobriety on social media again. With each post I'd make, the fear of judgment would fill my being.

It wasn't just the fear of being judged, but it was an odd fear of being shamed for trying to shine a bright light on the world of sobriety. As each day went on, I'd post consistently about drinking or a video of a statistic about alcohol. My following continued to grow. Yet, as each week went by, I'd still have that familiar fear that I was doing something wrong, or that I should be ashamed of my past. But, with each fear, oddly enough, I would get a message from a random stranger telling me that my posts helped them in some way, or that I was doing God's work.

As I've become more vocal about the transformational aspects that sobriety has in my life, the more opportunities I see to bring that light to those in need. Without sobriety, I never would have found my passion: helping people when they're at their lowest.

CHAPTER 10

ONE DAY AT A TIME

"We are what we repeatedly do. Excellence, therefore, is not an act,
but a habit."
Aristotle

When I thought about living a sober life, a concrete plan didn't come together at once. We're humans, not puzzles. When we change something, it may take some time before we can put the pieces of our lives back together again.

I was tempted on my first day of sobriety to think, "I'm never going to drink again," but realized that getting sober didn't require that long-term view. It required that I not drink. Today, for me and many others, it winds up being true that we never drink again. As you start down this path for yourself, I encourage you to not think years, weeks, or months down the road, but days. One day at a time is a motto that should be ingrained in everyone seeking to change any aspect of their life for the better.

When that feels like too much, take a deep breath, and live one moment at a time. A marathon breaks down into many individual steps. You'll never hit the finish line without taking that first step.

If you join me on this sober journey, it's going to be easy to get overwhelmed and second guess your decision. You might think that you're not good enough. That you're not strong enough. But the truth is that you don't have to be strong, or good enough. Give what you can at that moment and make the choice. It's not about perfection but progress. Surround yourself with those who will support you. Read up on the experiences of others.

So many people who struggle with alcohol look back on low points they wish could be erased from their lives. There are words you can't take back, actions you cannot delete, and time you'll never replace.

But life isn't about replacing the bad with the good. It's not about forgetting where you came from. Life is about acknowledging that we are imperfect beings. And through God, our faith can lead us on amazing adventures if we simply take the first step.

You'll eventually wake up with a smile on your face. You'll look at your life, and wonder: how did I get here?

Many times the greatest pain that I can associate with drinking is the feeling of dread and panic that would fill my mind the morning after. What did I do? What did I say? Omg, why can't I remember?!

When you choose a sober lifestyle, your energy increases. Your mood improves. You lose a little weight. Your health improves. Your relationships improve. It's like the part of Aladdin, "Genie, you're free!'"

But, everything worth having in life, is worth fighting for. While there are plenty of challenges that will await the person that desires sobriety, through determination, support, and persistence, you can achieve it.

Don't judge…we're all trying to do our best

It can be tempting to judge others who may be failing or struggling with sobriety. But this is wrong. Early on in sobriety we can get tunnel vision and think the sober way is the only way, but it's not. It's one way. For those that are called this way, it can be freeing and rewarding. I think it's a normal response to question other people's drinking early on in your sobriety because you're trying to justify your behavior or adjust to your new way of life. Instead of passing judgment on others, try to be there for them. Everyone you meet is struggling with something.

If their demon is alcohol or drugs, there is something behind the scenes that is probably propelling them onto that hardship. If you're able to lift the load and assist them along their way, then do that. If you can't do anything to ease their burdens, a kind word goes a long way. Sometimes, being an example of sobriety is the best thing you can do.

CHAPTER 11

FOR THE FAMILIES OR LOVED ONES OF SOMEONE STRUGGLING

"There is nothing noble in being superior to your fellow man; true nobility is being superior to your former self."
—Ernest Hemingway

For those who have been there for the pains and struggles of a loved one, my heart goes out to you. I wish there was something I could tell you that could lift the burden off your shoulders. Maybe you're seeing a loved one drink their life away. Maybe you're seeing them lose job opportunities, relationships, or friends because of their drinking. Maybe their drinking scares you and makes you worry if they are safe. Whatever the reason, thank you for feeling that love. Without love, you wouldn't be reading this book. Without love, you wouldn't see the person struggling as more than just a drunk, but a family member, a friend, and a confidant. Whatever your reason for reading this book, thank you for giving me a chance to inform, inspire and guide your journey to hope and healing. Thank you for believing that love can conquer all, you wouldn't be reading this book if you didn't believe on some level that there is hope that your loved one can quit drinking.

I can't imagine what you're going through. You may feel powerless. You may feel weak.

The advice I have for you is to be there for them. Be present to them. Express your love to them. Let them know you support them and want the best for them. While I have never been involved in an intervention, I believe there is a time and place for anything.

While it may be tempting to force your loved one to quit drinking, for me, it had to be a choice. I had to realize that alcohol wasn't good for me. I had quit before because others encouraged me, and it didn't last. The person needing sobriety needs to understand their why. Why are they getting sober? Why will they stay sober? Why is their amount of drinking bad? Why is alcohol bad for them?

Once that person understands why they shouldn't drink, they can begin to see a life without it. But also get help from AlAnon and other organizations that support family members. Self-care, in the long run, will help not only you but your loved one also. You are not being selfish by setting consequences and distancing yourself from the active drinker who is damaging the lives of those around them.

The best thing my wife did for me was love me. She loved me so much. And sometimes loving someone means saying "enough, I can't go on living like this." Consequences often work, and so does the power of love that dispels shame. I feel such great shame for the person that I was when I was drinking. For the drunken arguments, the bad behavior, everything. Nothing can take away that feeling of guilt or shame. However, a life of changed behavior, a life filled with positive moments, a life of redemption, can show that you can change. You can get better.

CHAPTER 12

IN CONCLUSION: SAME QUESTION. SAME ANSWER

"Conquer yourself, not the world"
-Rene Descarte

I still have nightmares from time to time. Dreams where I'm drinking and acting a fool. The feeling of regret consumes me. The feeling of guilt. The pain of failure. Yet, when I wake up, I realize quickly that it was just a dream. I take a deep sigh of relief, and I look at my life. I am filled with so much gratitude.

In the early days of sobriety, I reflected a lot on WHY I should quit drinking, or why I'm going to quit drinking. Everything was so fresh. That "why" stays with you. It stings. It doesn't let you forget where you came from, for fear of going back.

The struggle with being an alcoholic, or abusing alcohol, is that one drink is never enough. I know for a fact that while I am a person with a ton of self-discipline, I know that if I pour myself a glass of wine, I'll already be eying the rest of the bottle(s).

You may look back at my story and think it all happened just as planned and worked out perfectly. Yet my story, like many others, was filled with pain, sorrow, joy, fear, anxiety, happiness, and hope. We are imperfect beings, and no story is perfect. We aren't some fairy tale character that always lives happily ever after. But I do believe for those that can find the courage and bravery to face their challenges head-on, miraculous things can happen. While I can't promise you the sober life will be easy, I can promise you that you will never regret giving up alcohol once you experience the healing grace of sobriety.

We can change. We can transform our lives. But the question is still the same. "Why did I quit drinking?" The answer usually echoes throughout your life: because I chose to be a better me.

Life happens so quickly and while we can't change our past, we can for sure change our future. It all starts today, with a choice, with one step.

At the end of the day, the adjustment to a sober life requires you to take a good long look at yourself in the mirror.

To see your flaws, your failures, but also the beauty and the amazing potential that's in front of you. Take notice of your past, and make amends where possible, but give yourself some time to adjust. You're about to make the biggest change of your life, and you're going to look back at this moment down the road and be so extremely grateful you made this choice to be sober.

Now go, I believe in you! Take charge of your life, live to your fullest, and be the best damn person you can be.

-Charlie

APPENDIX A

FREQUENTLY ASKED QUESTIONS

Since becoming sober, I get asked similar questions by many people. I thought it would be helpful to add a Frequently Asked Question section for this book. These are the personal responses I typically share.

How do you adjust to your new life?

Don't put too much pressure on yourself. You've made the choice and commitment to be sober and that's huge. The 12-step program has a great saying: "Take it one day at a time", and when that's too much, take it "One moment at a time"

Was getting sober hard?

Hard? It's different. I think any time we try to change something in our lives that we've grown accustomed to, or grown addicted to, it can be difficult to change our behaviors. With something like alcohol abuse, drinking does not only affect what we drink but how we act, how we think, how we feel, how we sleep, how we look, everything. So, when you make a change to become sober, many things will change in your life. But I promise you, that for every sucky or hard moment, there will be 10 times as many awesome moments. Just because something may seem hard, doesn't mean it isn't worth it.

Does it get easier?

Let's go back to the analogy of learning to ride a bike without training wheels. Do you worry about riding a bike now? No, you have confidence in your cycling ability. The same thing happens with abstaining from alcohol. Since there are so many changes early on, once you get comfortable in your new skin, things do seem easier. But, just because they may seem easier, doesn't take away the temptation to drink, or that desire. It's something you must always be vigilant against.

Were people supportive?

Yes and no. My wife and those closest to me were the most supportive. But, don't go into sobriety expecting that everyone is going to be excited for you. Because the reality is that many more people are struggling with alcohol than care to admit it. And your sobriety may make them check themselves and they're drinking. But, those that mattered in my life, were super supportive. My wife is a saint.

Throughout my struggles, she loved me, she saw me for me, and she supported me. The best way to say you're sorry for drinking or other things is to change your behavior.

Did you lose friends?

I don't think I lost friends. I lost drinking buddies in my life. There's an old phrase that says you'll never be alone at a bar if you need someone to talk to. There are plenty of people in the world that struggle with alcohol, or use it to numb reality. While I may have lost "connection" with people in my life that I thought were my friends, the reality is that they were just acquaintances that liked drinking with me. There's a difference. And on your road to sobriety, you'll learn it.

Do you have issues with others drinking around you?

No. I'm a pretty self-disciplined person. Oddly enough, when I quit smoking many years prior, it was super tempting to want a cigarette when I was around others. But, with alcohol, it didn't tempt me to want to drink. So, while I may not have had issues with people drinking around me, I did have issues with people getting drunk around me. They say you go in phases of sobriety when you quit drinking. One of the earliest phases I went through was that I was super bored when I'd host get-togethers. I felt naked without my drink. I felt alone. I felt like I was missing a part of me that made me confident, that made me, me! I acknowledged that this was how I was feeling, and I knew I needed to do something different. So, if I'm not going to drink at a party, what can I do that's positive? So, I focused on being a great host.

Did it feel awkward telling people that you were sober?

I held it in for a while. I thought there was something wrong with me. I felt like a failure: why can't I just have ONE drink like everyone else? As the days, and weeks of sobriety go by, you start caring less and less about what other people think. You begin to appreciate the freedom you're experiencing. In the beginning, it was so foreign to me, so it was kinda hard to say it with confidence. I remember early on telling people I was on medicine that I can't drink on, and I made excuses for why I wasn't drinking. I'd say I'm on a diet, etc. Eventually, I got comfortable telling people I don't drink.

Do you miss it?

Sometimes. Granted, I've been sober since 2017, but in the beginning, I don't know if it was as much of a "missing" thing, as it was a void. Drinking alcohol allowed me to numb my feelings and escape reality. Eliminating alcohol made me aware of not only the void it filled but the reality that I'd need to change.

If you could go back and tell yourself something on the first day of sobriety, what would it be?

I am so proud of you. You have no idea how much this is going to change your life for the better. You will become a better husband, a better father, a better friend, and a better person. There are going to be plenty of highs and lows up ahead, so don't lose hope. You don't get to experience a rainbow till after the storm, and the rainbow is breathtaking.

How do you deal with social drinking situations as a sober person?

In the beginning, I thought people cared so much about me not drinking. I made it such a big deal in my mind. Early on I grew a fascination with sparkling water, so if I was out with friends that were drinking, I'd order sparkling water or a club soda. Your sobriety doesn't mean as much to other people as it does to you. And those that make a bigger deal of it than you, probably aren't going to be around you for long.

You said you struggled with social anxiety when you became sober, how did you get a handle on that?

Well, I never realized I struggled with social anxiety until I became sober. So, early on I would meet with a psychologist almost every week to discuss life, and get her support. Becoming sober is a change, and realizing I was hiding social anxiety with alcohol, made me feel super vulnerable and weak out there. But, through therapy, and my support group things got better over time. Initially, I would almost always have my wife or a close friend with me in larger social settings, I needed the support.

How long did it take for you to feel normal?

In the beginning, I felt like Aladdin a lot, it was all a whole new world. As the days went by I got more and more comfortable in my own skin. I don't know if there was a certain time frame it took to feel "normal", but eventually, it just makes sense, and you start to forget about the drinking person and realize you're the sober one.

APPENDIX B

MY GO-TO SOURCES OF INSPIRATION AT DIFFERENT PHASES ALONG THE WAY

These are the quotes, prayers, and phrases that I turned to at different phases of my sober journey

The Serenity Prayer became my best friend during the early days.

God grant me the serenity

To accept the things I cannot change;

Courage to change the things I can;

And wisdom to know the difference.

Living one day at a time;

Enjoying one moment at a time;

Accepting hardships as the pathway to peace;

Taking, as He did, this sinful world

As it is, not as I would have it;

Trusting that He will make things right

If I surrender to His Will;

So that I may be reasonably happy in this life

And supremely happy with Him

Forever and ever in the next.

~Amen~

"Just that you do the right thing.
The rest doesn't matter"

~Marcus Aurelius

"I shall pass this way but once; any good that I can do or any
kindness I can show to any human being; let me do it now.
Let me not defer nor neglect it, for I shall not pass this way
again."

~Etienne de Grellet

Saint Mother Teresa Prayer

People are often unreasonable, irrational, and self-centered. Forgive them anyway.

If you are kind, people may accuse you of selfish, ulterior motives. Be kind anyway.

If you are successful, you will win some unfaithful friends and some genuine enemies. Succeed anyway.

If you are honest and sincere people may deceive you. Be honest and sincere anyway.

What you spend years creating, others could destroy overnight. Create anyway.

If you find serenity and happiness, some may be jealous. Be happy anyway.

The good you do today, will often be forgotten. Do good anyway.

Give the best you have, and it will never be enough. Give your best anyway.

In the final analysis, it is between you and God. It was never between you and them anyway.

Suscipe
Take, Lord, and receive all my liberty,
My memory, my understanding, and my entire will,
All I have and call my own.
You have given all to me.
To you, Lord, I return it.
Everything is yours; do with it what you will,
Give me only your love and your grace,
That is enough for me.

~St. Ignatius Loyola

"To be a star, you must shine your own light, follow your path,
and don't worry about the darkness, for that is when the star
shines brightest. Also, do what you are afraid to do."

~Ralph Waldo Emerson

"Promise Yourself

To be so strong that nothing

can disturb your peace of mind.

To talk health, happiness, and prosperity

to every person you meet.

To make all your friends feel

that there is something in them

To look at the sunny side of everything

and make your optimism come true.

To think only the best, to work only for the best,

and to expect only the best.

To be just as enthusiastic about the success of others

as you are about your own.

To forget the mistakes of the past

and press on to the greater achievements of the future.

To wear a cheerful countenance at all times

and give every living creature you meet a smile.

To give so much time to the improvement of yourself

that you have no time to criticize others.

To be too large for worry, too noble for anger, too strong for fear,

and too happy to permit the presence of trouble.

To think well of yourself and to proclaim this fact to the world,

not in loud words but great deeds.

To live in faith that the whole world is on your side

so long as you are true to the best that is in you."

~Christian D. Larson

St. Michael the Archangel, defend us in battle.

Be our defense against the wickedness and snares of the Devil.

May God rebuke him, we humbly pray, and do thou,

O Prince of the heavenly hosts, by the power of God,

thrust into hell Satan, and all the evil spirits,

who prowl about the world seeking the ruin of souls.

~Amen~

Notes

Notes

~ 91 ~

Notes

~ 92 ~

Notes

Notes

~ 94 ~

Notes

~ 95 ~

Notes